POETIC SUNSHINE

SPLASH OF EMOTIONS

COMPILER & EDITOR

DEEPALI GANDHI

POETRY WORLD ORG

Copyright © POETRY WORLD ORG 2019

First Edition : 2019

<u>INDEX</u>

<u>HOPE</u>

By : Akshita Agrawal

Hey!
I know you are upset, but remember you are not the only
one who is not perfect.
People fall, people rise, but good nature is the only thing
that makes them wise.
Changes happen when we try, but if you're lost, just look
back to your every try.
I know that you are on your own, but I want you to know
that you're not alone.
Time makes everything come and go, but you know
what, just don't feel low.
You think you're going slow, but remember plants also
take time to grow.
Some people will pray for your failure, but don't feel sad
it's human behavior.
Keep going even though sometimes you will fall apart,
But don't worry different things come with different
start.
People will say things that don't matter, but eventually
things will get better.
So don't ever lose your hope, as you don't know but
there's still some scope.

<u>MAI CHALTE JAA RAHA HU</u>

By : Ankit Singh

Mai chalte jaa raha hu,

Ab rukne ka naam nahi,

Manzil ko pana hai,

Aur koi kaam nahi..

Thaana hai ye mann mein,

Kuch karke dikhana hai,

Chahe lakh mushkile aaye,

Bss ladte jaaana hai;

Badi chain ki roti todh liya,

Ab karna bilkul aaram nahi;

Mai chalte jaa raha hu,

Ab rukne ka naam nahi,

Manzil ko pana hai,

Aur koi kaam nahi..

Badi suni kahani manjhi ki,

Jhansi ki fateh purani hai;

Ab naam padhein sbb mera,
Kuch aisi baat banani hai;
Har jung fateh kar skta hai,
Aye bandeya tu aam nahi;
Mai chalte jaa raha hu,
Ab rukne ka naam nahi,
Manzil ko pana hai,
Aur koi kaam nahi..
Dil me arman bade,
Karne hai kaam bade;
Hatho pe hath rakhe,
Milte na naam bade;
Jago o mere bandhu,
Sone ka naam nahi;
Mai chalte jaa raha hu,
Ab rukne ka naam nahi,
Manzil ko pana hai,
Aur koi kaam nahi...

BRIGHT NIGHT

By: Arshi Acharya

Heaven full of stars,

Sequined the complete sky.

Outside the miragy bars,

The world glorifies.

Nox is nocturnal,

Cosmos is sleepy.

Ahead stands the brightest twinkle,

Upon the abyss stands divinity.

Here, dreams a soul,

Fantasies on eyelashes.

A million story to tell,

A heartfelt render chases.

Serenity of thus miasmal fair,

I cherish all alone.

My heart still wants to care,

Universe sorcerous prone.

<u>कभी - कभी</u>

By: Asha Avinash

ऐसा भी होता है कभी कभी

कुछ शब्दों में पूरा युग बयान होता है ,

सारा जीवन बीता सुनते, चारों ओर शोर ही शोर

चाँदनी रातों में भी अग्नि की हिलोर ।

ऐसा भी होता है कभी कभी

बसंत ऋतु में मन मयूर भी रोता है ,

न मालूम कब कहना पड़ जाये अंतिम प्रणाम

किस राह, किस पथ पर हो जाये जीवन तमाम ।

ऐसा भी होता है कभी कभी

जीवन भी साँसों पर प्राणों को ढोता है ,

पतझड़ वही होता है जहाँ हो बसंत

आदि तो अनिश्चित है, निश्चित है अंत ।

ऐसा भी होता है कभी कभी

पल भर जो समझौता है, वही जीवन होता है ।

<u>INDEPENDENCE</u>

By: Ayesha Shaikh

"What do you call an independent country?" I asked my
father one night.
He told me, "A country where you can do anything
following the rules of life,
Where everyone is treated equally, having all laws of
right,
Where no child sleeps hungry at night,
Where no one is arrested despite being correct at the
same time,
Where the husband has no right to slap his wife thinking
that she's fragile to reply.
Where the domestic walls are not only for women to
hide in,
Where you live without fear of being criticized,
Where books are not sold on the streets and respected
with much love and delight,
The truth is valued and valued more than the lies,

Where you do not have to shape your thoughts

according to the opinion of the society in disguise,

Where everyone is awake to do something special for

the country every time,

Not ever thinking about the return during life.

So I asked myself, are we free or just mighty

To get freedom at night in our beautiful dreams of

light?"

रेल सी जिंदगी

By: Basudeo Rajbhor

एक रेल सी हो चलि है जिंदगी,
जंग लग रही है फिर भी चले जा रहे हैं,
बूढ़े हो रहे हें फिर भी चले जा रहे हैं ।

लोग आते हैं जिंदगी में, चार बातें बनाते हैं,
कुछ किस्से सुनाते हैं, हंसते हैं रोते हैं,
और फिर एक दिन चले जाते हैं,
रोज़ का सफर बन गई है जिंदगी,
एक रेल सी हो चलि है जिंदगी ।

एक स्टेशन से दुसरे तक जाना है,
उसी बीच कूछ कमाना, कूछ गंवाना है,
ख़ाली ही शुरू हुई थी एक रेल के जैसे,
और आखिर स्टेशन पर खाली हो जाना है ।

मन करता है पटरियां बदल के देखूं,
कुछ नये रास्ते जाके देखूं, लेकिन,
कुछ ज़िमेदारीयों का बोझ हो चलि है जिंदगी,
एक रेल सी हो चलि है जिंदगी ।

<u>AGONY OF LOVE</u>

By : Bushra Shaikh (Saeraa)

Love, just a four letter word, and the emotions related to it are infinite; viz affection, tenderness, fondness, warmth, endearment, and so on. Love is not just a garden full of roses, it even has thorns which injures, causing deep wounds which are so intense that the damage can be felt by one's soul. You know, when we as individuals decide to take some immense torment be it physically or mentally for a long time, the consequences of such action drops down to zero. Be it pain, fear, strain, discomfort etc. the body doesn't react to it anymore, as it gets used to it. But there is something which the mind and heart always reacts to no matter how long the suffering persists is... "AGONY OF LOVE"

AGONY of LOVE or you can say "Pain - gain". You must have surely heard about that phrase "POISON KILLS POISON".

An individual might try the same for pain, "PAIN KILLS PAIN", oh it does not, not at least in love. Pain only goes on increasing, never settles down, just like love. Feeling affection or warmth towards anything cannot be controlled by one's mind or heart, same for pain, the suffering felt in love never fades, it surely reduces, or sorry, pretend to reduce but deep down, the damage it causes to the inner side is never known, it keeps coming up from time to time just to give one a slow and painful reminder. ANOGY has a specialty to cling on to the most sensitive elements viz emotions, memories, thoughts and so on.... Example:- Suddenly out of blue one might come across their favorite songs, place, food, activity or even a small word, actions, followed by memories and clinging on to that comes pain, which surely fades away with time but doesn't heal.

As time has the power to dwindle it, pain just wants one reason to bounce back again.. Out-coming in deepening the wound.
Only LOVE & FORGIVENESS sustains power to heal.
LOVE, as it has spiritual healing energies.
FORGIVENESS, is a key to set the soul free by releasing the burden, heaviness of the heart and unknotting the karmic depths.

"Love, is one of the most sacred feeling,

Love, has the powers to heal,

Love, never destroys,

It's the people and their pain,

Which causes damage.

Understand the difference...."

<u>VERSES ABOVE THE GROUND</u>

By: Carmelita Cruz Rivera

Verses above the cloud
Inside the plane, the small window is a frame of a picture
above the clouds
The haze of blue sky is an umbrella of illusion,
And a mirror of imagination, searching images of your
serious face,
Of your smiling eyes, of your slim body and all about
you.
Islands of white clouds tall and low, round and long,
thick or thin like the height of my hope,
But never low in trust.
Round is my infinite patience, long is my endless
waiting,
As thick as my coat of love and never thin with
forgiveness,
They're the shapes of my heart,
Wide sky in blue and gray,
Display of loneliness away from you,
Floating clouds of pure white as clean as my true
affection,
It's all about you and me.

I'M SCARED

By : Falguni Sarkar

I'm Scared of men.

I'm scared of those creepy DMs.

I'm scared of going out of my home.

I'm scared of everyone who looks at me.

I'm scared of my voice getting pressed due to someone's

influence.

I'm scared of saying NO to anyone.

I'm scared of everything that questions my character.

I'm scared of all the things happening around me.

I'm scared of being another Nirbhaya, Asifa, Madhu.

I'm scared of my existence.

Yes, I'm Scared.

Yes, I'm Scared!

<u>OCEANS</u>

By: Farheen Sha (The Scorp)

They think we have to sleep around,
To climb up the ladder.
That to match up to men,
We don't have enough calibre.

They think to get rich,
We have to marry wealthy husbands.
At the end of the day all we can do,
Is to run the household errands.

But we are oceans of wealth,
Full of opulence.
You envy our resources,
That's all there is to your sad existence.

They tell us we are less,
And that we should know our limits.
They try to show us our place,
And convince us that bearing children is our life's
summit.

But baby we are oceans of strength,
And you can't begin to measure our depth.
We can bear the children alright,
But we'll get back to business intact.

They think they can shame our bodies,
And objectify our private parts.
They think they'll get away with it,
Leaving us humiliated and torn apart.

But we are oceans of power,
Our curves are our waves.
One single breaker in your direction,
And you'll be stuck undercover for days.

They say we cry to gain sympathy,
Tears are our mightiest weapon.
Our existence is that of misery,
And when we weep we do our penance.

But we are oceans of emotions,
And our tears are in fact our biggest defense.
They're made of fire and ice,
And they'll dissolve you till you meet your very end.

<u>KOI OR HAI</u>

By : Garima Singh Dhaiya

Tu khwaish hai aasmano ki.. Tujhe stata koi or hai

Tu pedaish hai jin paemano ki.. Tujhe rulata koi or hai

Tu bandgi hai armano ki.. Tujhe yaad dilata koi or hai

Tu jindagi hai lakho ki.. Tujhe chu pata koi or hai

Tu koshish hai faryado ki.. Tujhe hasil krta koi or hai

Tu manjil hai kai khwabo ki.. Tujhe hsata koi or hai

Tu aasha hai sapno ki ..Tujhe juthlata koi or hai

Tu pagdandi hai karmo ki.. Tujhe behlata koi or hai

Tu wasta hai khushio ka..Tujhe hrata koi or hai

Tu rasta hai umeedo ka.. Tujhe bhulata koi or hai

Tu kashmkash hai jindagi ki.. Tujhe suljhata koi or hai

Tu mohabbat hai ek ajnabi ki.. Tera sath nibhata koi or

hai

Tera sath nibhata koi or hai

बस तु आगे बढ़ता जा

By: Gajendra Singh

ये तन्हाई का आलम है,मेरे दोस्त खुल कर जी इसे,

ना मिले तो ना सही,पर हस कर जी इसे ।

छोड दे सारे चिंतन तु , थाम ले उस मंजिल का रास्ता,

चलता जा-बस तु आगे चलता जा,उमड-घुमड कर बढता जा।

ना कर परवाह तु अपनी मंजिल प्राप्ति का,

लिखता जा बस तु लिखता जा इतिहास इस काल के कपाल पर

बस तु लिखता जा इतिहास।

ना कर चिन्तन तु आपनी सफलता का,

ना मिले तो ना सही, बस तु आगे बढ़ता जा ।

कर अपने हौसलो को बुलन्द निडर होकर चलता जा,

इस घने अंधकार में से अपने दीप बिखेरता जा,

बस तु आगे बढ़ता जा,बस तु आगे बढता जा ।

ना कर चिन्तन तु अपनी सुख प्राप्ति का ,

अपने आप से लड़ता जा बस तु आगे बढता जा ।

जिंदगी अभी अधुरी है, संकल्प भी अधुरा है,

गिर कर-संभल कर चलता जा, बस तु आगे बढता जा ।

एक दिन सितारा फिर झिलमिलायेगा,नया सेवरा फिर आएगा

उस दिन लोग तुझे तेरी उस इतिहास से जानेंगे जहाँ सिर्फ तुहि

तु नजर आएगा।

बस तु लडता जा मुस्कुराता जा, बस तु आगे बढ़ता जा ।

FROM A DISTANCE

By: Intajur Rahman

Certain heart touchy things are good from a distance,

The grass on the distance looks greenery,

The hill in the distance looks even,

The ocean in distance looks calm and quite,

And the prettiest face of yours, looks happier and

charming,

Until, I came close to you,

And discovered the thorns of the grass,

Hard rock of the hill,

Fast current stream of the Ocean,

And pain behind the pretty smile of yours.

<u>MIRROR IS MY BEST FRIEND</u>

By: Kiran Chetri

Mirror is my best friend
My words are expressed through pen,
But I told the story to mirror
People give me pain,
And never come to make me happy,
But mirror make me feel happy.
People told me how ugly I am
But mirror says how beautiful I am.
I hide my pain from others
But I express my innermost feelings to mirror,
When no one is there when I need
But mirror is always there for me
People judge me
But mirror never judges me.
Mirror never speaks
But says so many good things and advisable thoughts.
I know people come and go
But mirror never leaves my side
Mirror is my best friend
Mirror is my best friend forever.

<u>MY KIND OF LIFE</u>

By : Deepali Gandhi

Fairy tales are my kind,

The princess rock, the family is blind.

Independent thoughts, those love quotes,

Neither the king nor the kingdom knows.

Pretty gowns, beautiful looks,

They are not even supposed to cook.

Free life..own decisions,

No judgement..No revisions.

Handsome hunks themselves arrive,

Their lives and their kingdom thrives.

Endings are all done beautifully well,

Thereafter they happily dwell.

<u>HOPE</u>

By: Parinita Bhattacharjya

Why need of diamond to wear?
If you have your smile on your face.
That can beautify others too.

Why not to learn from children?
After fighting,
How they laugh and share together.

Why not to finish quarrel with love?
In place of finish love with quarrel.
Why to destroy peace for religion?
Wait, till then, when God will ask for your favor.

Why to continue misunderstanding?
In a field of sorry,
Can grow healthy seeds of relationship.

Why to break someone's heart?
If you can't measure the pain of bleeding heart.
Live...Love...Laugh...
3L s of caring trust.

मौन

By: Pawan Poddar

आँखें जो खुली तो उसे अपने करीब पाया ना था।
कभी थे उसकी ज़िन्दगी में शामिल
आज उनका साया ना था।
उसके दिल में कोई और है
यह उसने कभी बताया ना था।
बेपनाह मोहब्बत की जिससे
उससे उम्मीदें लिये बैठे थे।
उनसे तन्हाइयों की सौगातें मिलेंगी
यह किसीने बताया ना था।
एक हम ही उसकी आंखे हर बार पढ़ते रहे पर
मैंने तो कभी हाल-ए-दिल सुनाया ना था।
में फिरता रहा दिल में ना जाने कितने राज लिये
हमने तो कभी उनसे जज़्बातों को छुपाया ना था।
नाजाने क्यों हम बेवजह ही उससे बातें करते थे
हाल लफ़्ज़ों में तो उसने कभी बताया ना था।
कहीं कब्ज़ा कर रखा था दिलो के महल पर
मैंने वो ख़्वाब तो कभी आँखों में सजाए ना था।
धड़कन 'मौन' थी मेरी
जब एक आह की आवाज़ आई।
शिकवा क्या था मुझसे जो उसने
कभी अपना बनाया ना था।

<u>NIGHT IN THE JAR</u>

By: Priyal Vasoya

Have you ever tried capturing the night into a jar?

Or ever have you imagined if the stars could fly?

Would then they still fall?

For I want to ask them to fulfill plenty wishes.

Is it 'ok' to keep the moon half?

Just to save some room for the fireflies in the jar?

And I promise to keep the night's beauty.

<u>YOU</u>

By: Rajnandini Sahu

Many will come and many may go, but you have to go
on forever.

There's no limit, no rules, just a way you have to
choose.

Break the barriers, escape the hurdles, and take pride in
small adventures.

You are everything you need, and you have everything
in you to succeed.

Never lower down your self-confidence, do have some
forbearance.

Do you know who your biggest enemy is? You, yourself
are your enemy.

Think of doing better, think of being better every day.

For everyone who doesn't appreciate now, would surely
repent then.

You are strong, beautiful; you are the solace you search
for.

Find yourself and face the fear, be the influencer, be the
leader, Be You!

ज़िंदगी की कीमत

By: Raj Kumar Dangi

जाने कैसे लोग होते है जो इश्क़ के लिए अपनी जान देते है,

वो अपने माँ बाप को कैसे भूल जाते है जो उन्हें जीवन दान देते है!

इतना तो सोचते जो जीते जी नहीं मिला वो मरने के बाद कैसे मिलेगा,

तुम तो मर जाओगे पर तुम्हारा परिवार कितनो का मुँह सिलेगा!

तुम्हारी माँ ने तुम्हे चलना सिखाया और पापा ने तुम्हे पहचान दी,

कितने पागल थे तुम जो एक अजनबी के लिए अपनी जान दी !

अगर तुम्हे इतना प्यार करना ही था तो माँ बाप भाई बहन से करते,

इतनी ख़ुशी मिलती बस यही सोचते की हे भगवान इस जीवन में तो कभी ना मरते!

ये जो प्यार प्यार करते हो उसकी वजह तो जान लो,

उसके बाद तुम्हे समझ आएगा की ना अपनी जान दो और ना किसी की जान लो !

A MASK ON LOVE

By: Ruth Aishwarya

She threw love, he caught that love

Both played well.

After some days, her family distracted her,

She threw him,

He was melting daily with her thoughts.

After many years, still he was waiting for her.

But she was wearing a mask, for her heart and she was

cheating herself.

Still he was waiting for her.

She wipes her tears, and wiped him too.

In her heart, his love went beneath the mother's love.

She made her love 'end it all' and murdered his love.

Her pessimistic mind exceeds her optimistic heart.

Beautifully she make overed as a bad girl in front of

him.

But his true eyes were able to find the hidden face of

her.

But she doesn't want to remove her mask on love.

<u>THE DISGUISE</u>

By: Rushika Chawla

I started noticing the masks that people wore,

I felt too exposed to roam,

Where everybody was a mystery.

I felt myself to be like an open book,

I searched and searched to find someone like me there,

All I found was the veil that people wore.

I felt like holding on to someone better,

It was like a new phase altogether.

Look! I yelled to myself,

There is some goodness still left.

The human that was real,

Was like a rose in a garden full of thorns,

And fortuitously I, a sunflower had met him.

He felt like the new tilted earth ready to be sown,

He felt like a pollution free, fresh air.

Though the goodness within him wasn't enough,

I made him bleed through his own barb.

I turned my back to him when I saw sunlight,

After all, I was a mere sunflower using the rose at
nights.
Days later, I saw him in a facade.
No sooner did I realize,
Nobody was fake, except the people I know,
They were all withholding themselves from bleeding
through my cruel ways.
I was the one wearing the mask all along.

प्रेम.. हकीकत या फसाना

By: Shubh Shree

प्यार शब्द एक छलावा है, दुनिया को इसने भरमाया है,,

दिल में छोटी सी आश जगाकर, रोना ही इसने सिर्फ सिखाया है।

उम्मीद लगा के अपनों से, अपनों की असलियत दिखाया है,,

चाहत की डोर बांध कर , मायाजाल बिछाया है।

सुलझाने की कोशिश कोइ करें अगर , हकीकत से रूबरू हो गए अगर,,

पिंजर की कैद से आजादी उसी ने पाया है।।

एक पहल की जिसने हकीकत से मिलने की, आगे उसने यश कमाया है,,

पर किसी ने नहीं झांक कर देखा अंदर, कितनी खाई उसकी हृदय में बन आया है।

ढूंढ कर देखा जब उसने मरहम दर्द का, क्या हास्यास्पद थी वह घड़ी,,

जब उसने प्रेम को ही अपना उपचार पाया है।।

प्रेम.. हकीकत या फसाना

I CALL IT AS

By: Sneha.S

I am not the same
With my respite, inappreciable.
The irony of my ideology,
leaves me bewildered.
"What if's" exist in my entire context,
Imbibing all my bliss.
Striking on the other side
of the match stick
my mind apologies,
For the hangover.
But still the reason behind,
remains inexplicable.
The door for my thoughts
are neither open nor close,
but seems to be unbuilt.
Thoughts turned into wanderlust.
Giving me the intolerable perk
Of staying idle.
What should I call this as?
"Over thinking?"

<u>LIFE LESSON</u>

By: Sumaiya Nadeem

Oh, I had insecurities all right,

Bottled up the emotions all night.

Liars for friends I got all the time,

Times when I was naïve.

Never realized people stabbed me in the back,

Crushed my trust and walked away.

I would just stand aside and give them way.

Why didn't I realize my self worth?

I thought, I was no one in this popularity-based world.

Went through pain both physical and mental,

But never showed people that the struggle is real.

Those times taught me a life lesson- People never see

your struggle,

They only judge you on your achievements.

According to them, if you don't show your flare once,

That means you have never shone.

So don't listen to what they have to say,

Do what you want to do, have it your way.

<u>मैं 'मैं' हूं</u>

By : Swati Tripathi

मैं 'मैं' हूं

लफ़्ज़ों में उलझी

खामोशियों से कहती,

आइने के सामने

सपनों को बुनती,

जीने की ख़ाहिश में

अपनो से लड़ती,

स्वाभिमान की आंच में

खुद ही झुलसती,

कपड़ो की लंबाई से

खुद को ढकती,

नज़रो की चोट से

कोशिश बचने की करती,

ख़्वाबों से बाहर

हक़ीकत से मिलती,

ज़िंदगी जीने का संघर्ष

आज भी करती.....

यादे

By : Yagnesh Parmar

यूँ चुप रहने से कभी अल्फाज़ भी खत्म हो जाते है,

बिना बाते करने से कभी अहसास भी कम हो जाते हे,

खामोशियों के दौर मे हर लम्हे ऐसे ही कट जाते हे,

तब खुशियो के पल बिताने कुछ लोग बहोत याद आते है

MOTIVATIONAL QUOTE

By: M.V.Alagubalasingaram

Better place makes a man better and comfort,
but only a better person can make that place more better
and valuable.